Holiday in the Rain Forest

and

Kabuki Gift

Two Original Plays

Holiday in the Rain Forest

and

Kabuki Gift

Two Original Plays

by Douglas Love

HarperCollins*Publishers*

Library of Congress Cataloging-in-Publication Data
Love, Douglas.
  [Holiday in the rain forest]
  Holiday in the rain forest ; and Kabuki gift : two original plays / by Douglas Love
    p.   cm.
  Summary: Two plays, one about a family's environmentally enlightening vacation, and the other, set in ancient Japan, combining the style of Kabuki theater with modern American humor.
  ISBN 0-06-024276-0 (lib. bdg.)
  1. Children's plays, American.   [1. Environmental protection—Drama.
2. Japan—Drama   3. Plays]   I. Love, Douglas. Kabuki gift.   II. Title
III. Title: Holiday in the rain forest. IV. Title: Kabuki gift.
PS3562.O839H65   1994
812'.54—dc20   93-41615
                                                               CIP
                                                               AC

1   2   3   4   5   6   7   8   9   10
First Edition
❖

Holiday in the Rain Forest *is for Martha.*

Kabuki Gift *is for my most honorable friends Gretta, Sharon, Jamie, Todd, and Norrice.*

Contents

Introduction

The first time I stepped inside a theater, I thought that it was the most magical place in the world. I went with my class to see a show at the performing arts center in my town. It was a musical for children produced by a professional company of actors. I was immediately captivated. Right there in front of me, performers were singing and dancing and telling a story—live! It seemed that they were talking directly to me, and I was completely enthralled with the characters and their adventures. The sets and costumes weren't fancy or extravagant, but this made me even more involved in the production. I was able to use my imagination to pick up where the limitations of the sets and costumes left off. This first production was my introduction to the world of theater.

You are about to embark on an exciting adventure. Planning, rehearsing, and staging a play can be a fun and satisfying experience. It's up to you to make your play the best it can be. The written script is only the beginning. It is meant to be used like a map, a route that guides you through the story.

Because actors in a play are right in front of an audience (not up on a movie screen or inside a television), anything can happen, and it usually does. Scenery may fall over, people may say the wrong lines at the wrong time or forget their lines altogether. When these mistakes happen, the actors can't stop and start over. In the theater, they go right on and try to get back on track with as much ease as possible. This is the challenge of live theater. The feeling that *anything can happen* keeps everyone on their toes.

While working on your production, don't be discouraged if you feel that you don't have the exact prop or costume that the play calls for. If the stage directions ask for a couch in a certain scene, there is no rule that says you can't use a bench, or a chair, or nothing at all instead. You should decide what you think is important to include. Some of the best plays have no props or stage settings at all. The audience is able to use its imagination. That can be fun for the audience!

It is almost always helpful to have someone serve as the director of the play, whether you are performing in your school or your backyard. This person will help make decisions about the direction your production takes: Will everyone wear costumes? Will you make a set? Who will play which character? He or she may also designate certain parts of the stage to be different places where the action takes place. The director should also help everyone working on the play realize that theater is a collaborative art. This means that the talents of a lot of people come together to create one exciting production that everyone can be proud of because everyone helped to create it.

Performers have a special task in the play. When you know what role you will play, the next step is to develop your character. This is achieved by asking yourself a lot of questions: If I was this person (or animal), how would I walk? How would I stand? How would I speak? What would I wear? Whom do I like in the play? Whom don't I like? What do I want to do in the play? You can and should ask yourself these and more questions about your character. Then, you have to answer these questions and make some decisions. If you are playing an old man, you might decide to stand hunched over and walk with a cane. You may choose to have a gravelly voice and tattered clothes. You may discover while reading the play that you are a rich old man who doesn't spend any of his money, and you are afraid that everyone is trying to steal it.

The answers and decisions that you make about your character are guideposts on your journey. It's okay to change your mind if something isn't working. None of the choices that you make for your character are wrong. Experiment! That's what rehearsals are for. Refer to the performance tips before each play for some suggestions.

Rehearsal is extremely important if you plan to perform your play for an audience. Some theater directors and actors believe that you should rehearse one hour for every minute that you are onstage. Some of that rehearsal time can be spent on your own, memorizing your lines. Different people memorize lines differently, but all techniques have one thing in common—repetition. Go over and over and over your lines until you can say them without looking at the script. Some people sit alone reading their lines again and again until they can say them from memory. Others read their lines into a tape recorder and listen to the tape over and over. Or ask a friend or someone in your family to "hold book." This means that they read the line that comes before yours and then you say your line.

Rehearsal is also the time to decide on your blocking, or the physical action of the play. Who does what, when? If everything is planned before the performance, you'll feel more secure, and the audience will be able to follow the story more easily.

When planning your blocking, remember that you are performing for an audience that needs to see what is going on to follow the story of the play. Important action should take place closer to the audience. Try to face the audience as much as possible; this allows them to see your facial expressions and hear you better.

Whether you will be performing on your school stage, in your classroom, or at home, feel free to make changes to make the play work for you, and use them as a jumping off point into the unlimited world of your own creativity and imagination.

About *Holiday in the Rain Forest*

You'll want to keep the following performance tips in mind if you're putting on your own production of *Holiday in the Rain Forest*.

The Characters

The following descriptions of the characters in *Holiday in the Rain Forest* are just a starting point. It is up to you to fully develop your own character by reading the play carefully, and forming your own opinion of your character's personality.

Frannie Kane is the mom in the Kane family. At first she wants to show off and impress her friends. She eventually learns that there are more important things than showing off vacation slides.

Manny Kane is the dad in the Kane family.

Anne Kane is Frannie and Manny's 11-year-old daughter. She likes to figure things out for herself.

Gilbert Kane is Frannie and Manny's 10-year-old son. He is often bored—until he gets to the rain forest.

Ray is the multipersonality worker at the rain forest motel. Every time he changes his hat and becomes someone else, he should also change the way that he stands, moves, and talks!

Gladys Montrose lives with her husband and children near the Kanes. She is very concerned with outdoing her neighbors.

George Montrose is Gladys's husband. He is also very concerned with appearances and material things.

Ginny and **Winny Montrose** are George and Gladys's twin daughters. They are spoiled and are constantly arguing.

Spike Montrose is the Montroses' baby. Spike is very demanding and loud.

Jack and **Melvin** are wisecracking, good-hearted alligators. They are like an old-fashioned comedy team. They laugh at each other's jokes harder than anyone else, even though they have already heard the jokes many times.

Ti is a tiny, beautiful butterfly. Ti cares about the stone people and genuinely wants to help them.

Rontihowa and **Antelo** are stone people who are very sensitive and caring. When they are brought back to life, they are full of wonder about their environment.

Chris Dayton, the talk-show host, is overly perky and full of smiles.

Sets and Props

As you read through the play, a picture will form in your mind of how a certain scene looks. Think about this picture, and how you can re-create it onstage through sets and props. The goal of sets and props is to give the audience a feeling for where the action is taking place.

Be observant. Pay close attention to things around you. What are five things that make your family's living room look like a living room? Use your imagination! How do you think a rain forest would look? What props can you add or take away to make the Kane's living room look very different from the lobby of Ray's Rain Forest Motel and Emporium?

Holiday in the Rain Forest takes place in a few different locations. There are two different living rooms, the Kanes' and the Montroses'. The Montroses' might have pictures on their walls or souvenirs that they've purchased on their vacations. Set up different configurations of chairs and tables to distinguish the two living-room areas. You might want to use the same furniture with different blankets or covers draped over them for the two different houses. If the furniture isn't arranged differently for the different houses, the audience might get confused.

The lobby of Ray's Rain Forest Motel and Emporium should have a desk that is large enough so the audience cannot see Ray when he ducks behind it. The desk should be cluttered with papers and office supplies.

The last scene takes place on the set of a television talk show. The characters should be sitting in a row of chairs across the stage, with Chris, the talk-show host, either standing or sitting on one end in a larger chair. She might carry a fake microphone.

Other props that you may need include telephones for the Kanes' and Montroses' living rooms, a camera, and four sleeping bags.

Cast

Frannie Kane
Manny Kane
Anne Kane
Gilbert Kane
Ray
Gladys Montrose
George Montrose
Winny Montrose
Ginny Montrose
Spike Montrose
Jack the Alligator
Melvin the Alligator
Ti, a butterfly
Rontihowa, a stone person
Antelo, a stone person
Chris Dayton, a talk-show host

Optional Smaller Cast

Actor 1—Frannie Kane, Winny Montrose
Actor 2—Manny Kane
Actor 3—Anne Kane, Ginny Montrose
Actor 4—Gilbert Kane
Actor 5—Chris Dayton, Ti, Spike Montrose
Actor 6—George Montrose, Melvin, Antelo, Ray
Actor 7—Gladys Montrose, Jack, Rontihowa

Scene 1

★ *We are inside the* KANES' *house. The stage is set to be a living room. A couch is placed on an angle left of center stage. A chair right of center faces the couch. There is a table with a lamp, phone, and answering machine. There are plastic food bags and empty soda cans spread throughout the set. The front door is offstage left.*

★ FRANNIE KANE, *a woman in her forties who is very concerned about what other people think, enters.* MANNY KANE, FRANNIE's *husband, also in his forties, enters with* FRANNIE. *Both are wearing hats, coats, and scarves.*

Frannie: That's it! *(fuming as she crosses to the couch)* That Gladys Montrose makes me so mad!

Manny *(taking off his coat)*: I can't ever remember being so bored in my life.

Frannie *(taking off her coat)*: The way they carried on!

Manny: Couldn't get a word in edgewise.

Frannie: How could they possibly think that we enjoyed ourselves this evening?

Manny: Is that their idea of entertaining?

Frannie: Is that their idea of a relaxing evening with friends?

9

Both *(together)*: Vacation slides!

Frannie *(mimicking)*: Pedro was our guide to the ancient city.

Manny *(also mimicking)*: The food was top rate, can't get anything like it in the States.

Frannie: Then when she started speaking with an accent and rolling her Rs!

Manny: And when he took out that big hat and started to dance!

Both *(together)*: WHAT A BORE! *(long pause)*

Frannie *(looking around the room)*: Will you look at this place? Those kids! It looks like a tornado hit.

Manny: I'll clean it up, dear. *(He gets up to clean. FRANNIE remains on the couch.)* Where are the paper bags?

Frannie: Oh, I throw those away. I have some plastic bags in the corner, there.

★ *MANNY begins to pick up garbage, throwing it into the plastic bag.*

Manny: What about these cans? Should I separate them?

Frannie: Separate them? They all end up in the same place! *(thinking)* Don't they? *(thinking more)* Honey? Where does all of this garbage end up, anyway?

Manny: In the garbage truck!

Frannie: Oh, of course! I almost forgot.

★ *MANNY continues to pick up garbage and place it all into one bag.*

Frannie: Honey? Why don't we take the kids to Mexico?

Manny: We just went on vacation!

Frannie: Just went? Where?

Manny: That amusement park with the rides and cartoon characters walking around.

Frannie: Amusement park?! You mean the rocking horse in the parking lot of the A & P with the bag boys who have to wear duck costumes?

Manny: The kids loved it.

Frannie: Gilbert threw up all over Dippy the Duck.

Manny: But he had fun!

Frannie: More than I can say for the duck. Oh, Manny, let's go away. What I wouldn't give to bore Gladys and George with our slides.

Manny: I think I've got some shots of Dippy.

Frannie: Please, Manny? Let's take the kids somewhere exotic.

Manny: Where?

Frannie: It has to be a place that none of our friends have gone.

Manny: I'm not going to the North Pole!

Frannie: Oh, no . . . the Jeffersons went there last Christmas. Now let's see, we can't go to Greece. The Andropolises went to Greece.

Manny: Italy?

Frannie: No, the Jorgensons went to Italy.

Manny: Ireland?

Frannie: The Peabodys went to Ireland.

Manny: China?

Frannie: No, no! The Georges had Sara's sweet sixteen in China. *(pause)* I know. . . Brazil! Oh, yes! Brazil! That's perfect! We could take trips into the wilderness! We could really "rough it"!

Manny: I'll pick up some travel books tomorrow!

★ *Blackout*

Scene 2

★ *Same location the next night.* FRANNIE *is looking through a brochure.* MANNY *is on the telephone.*

Manny *(on the phone)*: Hello? . . . Hello?! Is this Ray's Rain Forest Motel and Emporium? *(pause)* It is? Oh, great! Great! Now, are you located right in the heart of the rain forest? *(pause)* You're not? How far? *(pause)* A forty-five minute hike?

Frannie *(getting excited)*: Hike? Oh, a hike! *(calling offstage)* Did you hear that, kids? We're going to hike!

Manny: Yes. There are four of us, and the name is Kane. Now, we really want to "rough it"! We're looking for an adventure, or at least some really good photo opportunities! We'll be there Thursday! Good-bye.

Frannie: This is too much! Too much! Wait until I tell Gladys Montrose that we're going to the rain forest of South America! *(She crosses to the phone, then stops herself.)* No! I'll let them call us and get the answering machine!

Manny *(yelling offstage)*: Kids! Are you all packed?

★ ANNE, *eleven years old, enters wearing a frilly dress.*

Anne *(entering the stage from her room)*: Pretty much. Should I pack a dress?

Manny: A dress? No, honey, we're "roughing it"!

Frannie: You never know, dear. Maybe you'll need a dress. They may have a nice restaurant at the motel. After all, it is an emporium!

Manny: Then I better take a tie and jacket.

Frannie (*calling offstage to* GILBERT): Gilbert, make sure you pack a tie!

★ GILBERT, *ten years old, is dressed in jeans, T-shirt, and sneakers.*

Gilbert (*entering from his room, carrying a big stack of newspapers*): Do I have to?

Frannie: Yes, dear, you have to. Honestly!

Gilbert: Mom, what should I do with all of these newspapers I used for my social-studies project?

Frannie: Just throw them in with the garbage. I don't want them cluttering up the house! Get rid of them.

Anne: Mom, should I pack a raincoat?

Frannie: Oh, no, dear. "Rain" forest is just a figure of speech. It doesn't actually rain there.

★ *Blackout*

Scene 3

★ *The lobby of Ray's Rain Forest Motel and Emporium.
There is a chair downstage left and a motel check-in desk
upstage right.* RAY, *the motel owner, enters. Each time the*
KANES *ask to speak to someone else,* RAY *ducks behind the
desk and changes his hat to become the new character.*

★ RAY *walks behind the check-in desk and disappears
behind it.*

★ FRANNIE, MANNY, ANNE, *and* GILBERT *enter completely
drenched from the rain.*

Anne: I am completely soaked!

Gilbert *(shivering)*: I'm freezing!

Manny *(mimicking* FRANNIE*)*: "Rain" forest is just a
figure of speech!

Frannie: So I made a mistake! You've never made a
mistake? Besides, we've just had our very first
experience in "roughing it."

Manny: Mom's right, kids. Now we're at the motel. We
can dry off and change our clothes. I'll check us in.

★ MANNY *walks over to the check-in desk and rings the
service bell.* RAY *pops up from behind the desk.*

15

Ray: Hello. I'm Ray, the desk clerk. Welcome to Ray's Rain Forest Motel and Emporium. How may I help you?

Manny: We have reservations. Our name is Kane.

Ray *(looking through stacks of disorganized papers)*: Hmm. Kane, Kane. *(to MANNY)* Kane?

Manny: Yes, Kane.

Ray *(back to his papers)*: Hmm. Kane, Kane.

Manny *(becoming impatient)*: I don't understand this! We made the reservation just last week.

Frannie *(crossing to MANNY)*: Is there something wrong?

Manny: This guy can't find our reservation.

Frannie: What do you mean, he can't find our reservation? You made it last week. I heard you. *(to RAY)* I heard him!

Manny: Who's in charge here?

Ray: That would be Ray, the manager.

Manny: Then, I want to speak with Ray the manager.

★ RAY *ducks down behind the desk and reappears wearing a new hat.*

Ray: Can I help you folks?

Manny: No, no. We'll wait for the manager.

Ray: I am the manager. My name is Ray. Can I help you?

Manny: You're the manager?

Ray: Yes.

Manny: Why didn't you say that before?

Ray: Before what?

Manny: Before, when we first tried to check in.

Ray: That was Ray, the desk clerk. He told me that you folks needed my assistance.

Manny: Ray the desk clerk?

Ray: Yes.

Frannie: You're Ray the manager?

Ray: Yes . . . and your name?

★ *FRANNIE and MANNY look at each other and shrug.*

Manny: The name's Kane.

Ray *(looking through the papers)*: Kane. . . Kane . . . No. No Kane listed. Sorry.

Frannie: We have to be listed. We just called last week!

Ray: You called last week? Well, then. That explains it!

Manny: Explains what?

Ray: Ray, the new guy, was answering the phone last week.

Frannie: Ray the new guy?

Ray: Just hired him. He was messing up everything! Hold on, I'll get him. *(He ducks under the desk to retrieve a new hat, and emerges as RAY the new guy.)* Hi! I'm Ray the new guy. Ray the manager said that you needed my help?

Manny: You're Ray the new guy?

Frannie: You're Ray the new guy?

Ray: Wow! I never realized that there was an echo in here! Ray said you guys called last week? What's your name?

Manny *(running out of patience)*: KANE.

Ray: Let's just take a little look in the file.

Manny: They've already looked in the file and we're not there.

Ray *(finding the piece of paper)*: Here you are, under "L."

Frannie: "L"?

Ray: For "Last week"!

Manny: We don't care! We've been traveling all day. We are drenched and very tired. Which room are we in?

Ray: Which room? We've only got one room.

Frannie: One room? Is it vacant?

Ray: Sure it is. Nobody's ever stayed here. Not many people come to the rain forest for vacation. I'll call Ray the bellboy to get your bags. *(He gets another hat to become RAY the bellboy.)* Hello, sir. Which room are you in?

Manny: You've only got one room!

Ray: But of course. This way please.

★ *He leads the family offstage.*

★ *Blackout*

Scene 4

★ *The motel room at Ray's Rain Forest Motel and Emporium.* RAY *leads* FRANNIE, MANNY, GILBERT, *and* ANNE *to an empty room with sleeping bags rolled up in the center.*

Ray: Here you are. Home away from home!

Frannie: Your brochure said "lovely, spacious rooms."

Ray: You have to admit, there's lots of room in here!

Manny: That's because there's no furniture.

Gilbert: Where's the bathroom?

Ray: Well, do you see that tree over there?

Frannie *(looking out the window)*: Yes.

Ray: Turn left.

Manny: Now that's "roughing it."

Ray: Well, folks, my day's done. I'm going home. If you need anything . . .

Frannie: Let me guess. . . Ray the night clerk, right?

Ray: Oh, no. Pops watches the place at night. If you need anything, just ask him. He'll help you out. Good night.

★ *RAY exits.*

Anne: I don't like this place.

Gilbert: I want to go home.

Frannie: Now, kids, this is our family adventure. Our hotel room may not be fancy, but we've come here to "rough it." At least we have a room. Now, let's unpack and change into some dry clothes and go to bed.

Anne *(opening a suitcase)*: This isn't our stuff.

Frannie: What do you mean, this isn't our stuff? *(She looks at the clothes.)* Manny, this isn't our stuff.

Manny *(opening another suitcase)*: We must have picked up the wrong bags.

Frannie: Well, we have to get out of these wet clothes.

Gilbert *(taking a tunic-style costume out of one suitcase)*: These clothes look weird.

Manny: This must be what people wear around here.

Frannie: Just think of the great pictures we can take in these.

Manny: Okay, everybody. Change and go to bed. We've got a big day of pictures tomorrow.

Frannie: I'd give anything to see Gladys Montrose's face when she hears that we are vacationing in the South American rain forest!

★ *Blackout*

Scene 5

★ *The Montrose home.* GLADYS, *a woman in her late thirties, is on the phone.* GEORGE, *her husband, also late thirties, is reading the paper. With each page he finishes, he crinkles it up and puts it in a plastic bag.* SPIKE, *the baby, is in his playpen.*

Gladys: The South American what? George! George!

George: What is it, Gladys?

Gladys: Frannie and Manny are in the South American rain forest on vacation!

George: Big deal!

Gladys: That means that next year we'll have to go on some sort of safari.

George: If I know them, they'll want to show off and invite us to see some boring vacation slides when they get back.

Gladys: That would be just like them.

★ WINNY *enters with* GINNY, *her twin. Both are twelve years old and dressed alike.*

Winny: Mommy, Ginny stepped on my Italian shoes

that we got on our trip to Rome last year, and got them all dirty.

Ginny: Not before she stepped on my Mexican hat that we got from our vacation in Cancun.

George: Now you two go back to bed on your Swedish mattresses that we got on our vacation to Stockholm and wrap yourselves up in your Egyptian blankets that we got on our vacation to Cairo and go to sleep.

Ginny: That blanket makes me itch!

Gladys: It's not your blanket that itches. It's your yak-wool pajamas that we got you on our vacation to Tibet.

Ginny: Do I have to wear them?

George: Of course you do. They're a souvenir.

Winny: Mommy, did you find out where Anne and Gilbert went?

Gladys: Yes, dear. They went with their parents to the South American rain forest!

Winny: What's a rain forest?

George: It's sort of like a jungle.

Spike: Go to the rain forest! Go to the rain forest!

Ginny: Will they see real animals there?

Spike: See real animals! See real animals!

Winny: Why don't we ever go anywhere fun for vacation?

Spike: Go somewhere fun! Go somewhere fun!

Gladys *(impatiently)*: Spike, please! We go to lots of fun places!

Winny: Daddy, please let us come along to see the slides of the rain forest.

Spike: See slides! See slides!

George *(worn down)*: Okay, you can see the slides!

Gladys: Now, everyone go to bed! *(The twins help SPIKE out of the playpen and the three kids exit.)* If I know Frannie and Manny, they are probably in a fancy, beautiful hotel with lots of servants and nice restaurants.

George: That's the difference between us. If we were there, we'd really want to get a feel for things. We'd really "rough it."

★ *Blackout*

Scene 6

★ *The outskirts of the rain forest. The Kane family enters, stage left. They come upon two alligators, JACK and MELVIN.*

Anne *(to the alligators)*: Excuse me, we're looking for the rain forest. Do you know how to get there?

Jack *(teasing)*: The rain forest? GET IN LINE! *(to MELVIN)* You hear that, Melvin? These folks are looking for the rain forest!

Melvin *(laughing)*: The rain forest? What makes you think you can find the rain forest? Sitting here in this swamp, we see it all.

Jack: Last night, Melvin and I met a guy who was looking for the fountain of youth.

Melvin: Give it up. There's a broken dream for every lily pad on the swamp.

Frannie: Excuse me? Mister Alligator? Would you mind posing for a picture with my son?

Gilbert *(embarrassed)*: Ma!

Manny: Go on, son! It'll be cute.

Melvin: Now, pictures I do! How do I look, Jack? Do I

got any people stuck between my teeth?

★ *The family freezes in shock.*

Melvin: Just kidding!

★ *They all laugh nervously.*

Manny *(focusing the camera)*: Now, Gilbert, you get right in there with the alligator. Wait till Gladys and George see this one! Okay! Look fierce. *(He snaps the picture.)* Great shot!

Jack: All right, you got your picture, now go home!

Frannie: We can't go home! There are too many photo opportunities that we would miss. Besides, we've come a long way to see the rain forest.

Jack: Give me a break! Yeah, the rain forest used to come all the way out to this swamp. I guess that technically you are in the rain forest right now.

Anne: This isn't a forest. There aren't any trees here.

Melvin: Oh, this place was full of trees, once upon a time.

Manny: Once upon a time?

Melvin: They came through here and cut down all the trees around this swamp.

Gilbert: Why?

Jack: Farmers want the land, kid.

Frannie: Will the trees grow back?

Melvin: Trees don't grow back overnight. They haven't even replanted, and I'm not sure that they're planning to. To find the trees, you'll have to go near the mountains.

Manny (*looking at his map*): . . . and beyond the valleys?

Jack: You are already beyond the valleys.

Melvin: The mountains are far away. You have to travel on to see them.

Jack: Come with us. We will take you to the mountains.

Gilbert: Let's go!

★ *They move across the stage to the area that is at the edge of the mountains.*

Jack: Here we are. This is beyond the valleys and near the mountains.

★ *They all look around and see that there are still no trees.*

Frannie: There aren't any trees here either.

Melvin: They must have cut or burned these down, too.

Jack: They must be printing a lot of newspapers for you guys, with those trees.

Frannie: They aren't using these trees to make paper products that we use at home! We live very far from here.

Melvin: The paper made from the trees in the rain forest gets shipped all over the world.

Jack: Maybe there are some trees on the other side of the mountains. We can lead you to the edge of the swamp, but you're on your own after that.

★ *They all exit.*

★ *Blackout*

Scene 7

★ *The Land of the Stone People. The family comes across what appear to be statues of people. Two actors are standing centerstage, resembling statues. They wear drab gray-and-brown tunics and stand very still.*

Frannie *(yelling offstage to the alligators)*: Thanks! Take care!

Manny *(waving his camera)*: We'll send you copies of the snapshots!

Frannie: Bye!

Manny *(looking at all of the statues)*: WHAT IS THIS?

Gilbert: They look like statues.

Frannie: They don't look like any of the ancient heroes that I read about in the tour books.

Anne: Something is written on the side here.

Manny: What is it? What does it say?

Anne *(reading a small plaque next to* ANTELO *and* RONTIHOWA*)*: "Lost their hope—turned to stone."

Frannie *(puzzled)*: Lost their hope—turned to stone?

What does that mean? *(She looks at* MANNY *and smiles.)* Picture time!

★ *They all gather around a stone person while* MANNY *focuses.*

Gilbert: Look at this one! *(pointing to a statue)* Look at its eyes. They look very human.

Anne: You don't think these are people who have turned to stone, do you?

Frannie: Don't be silly! It is the artist's job to make the statue look real.

Gilbert: Well, this artist did a great job. This one is blinking!

Anne: Let's get out of here!

★ *They start to exit.* FRANNIE *stops them.*

Frannie: This is crazy! Statues don't blink!

★ *They look more closely at the statues.* MANNY *looks at his map.*

Gilbert: These statues are spooky. *(Looks closely at one of them.)* Their eyes look very lifelike. *(One of the stone people blinks.)* Did you see that?

Anne: See what?

Gilbert: That one! He moved his eyes!

★ *They all rush over.*

Manny *(to ANTELO)*: Can you hear us? Do you understand us?

★ ANTELO *blinks again, trying to communicate.*

Frannie *(to ANTELO)*: Are you alive? *(to MANNY)* He's moving his eyes—but he can't communicate with us! These are people, Manny! They're not statues!

Anne *(rereading the plaque)*: It says here, "Lost their hope—turned to stone." What could that mean, "Lost their hope"? I wonder what happened?

★ *Suddenly,* TI, *a butterfly, enters.*

Ti *(to MANNY)*: Hello.

Manny: Hello. Who are you?

Ti: I'm Ti. I'm a butterfly.

Frannie *(in a loud voice, as if TI doesn't understand English)*: GREETINGS! I AM FRANNIE. THIS IS MY HUSBAND, MANNY, AND OUR CHILDREN, GILBERT AND ANNE.

Ti: What are you doing here among these stones?

Anne *(to TI)*: These are people who have turned to stone!

Ti: Turned to stone? How did that happen?

Gilbert: We don't know. There's only this little sign here that says, "Lost their hope—turned to stone."

Ti: "Lost their hope"? What does that mean?

Anne: That was my question.

Frannie: Maybe if we gathered some fruits and berries and tried to feed them, they would come back to life.

Manny: Let's try it.

Anne: We have berries that we gathered on the trail up here with the alligators.

★ *They all take some of the fruits and berries from* ANNE *and try feeding* RONTIHOWA *and* ANTELO. *Nothing happens.*

Ti: It doesn't work. They're as stiff as they were when we began.

Gilbert *(thinking)*: "Lost their hope." Hmm. I wonder.

Ti: I have an idea. *(running off)* I'll be right back!

Anne: Where's she going?

Manny: I don't know. Look at her fly! Her wings are so beautiful and colorful.

Frannie *(looking up into the sky)*: Look, she's bringing others. Look at all those colors!

★ *The actors onstage look up above the heads of the*
audience and pretend to see the butterflies and birds.
They focus on the imaginary birds and butterflies
until RONTIHOWA *and* ANTELO *slowly come back to life.*
RONTIHOWA *and* ANTELO *slowly begin to move their*
heads, then arms, and finally legs.

Rontihowa: You have saved us. All of you! I am
Rontihowa, and this is Antelo. We wish to express our
gratitude.

Frannie: We're glad to help.

Manny: How did you lose your hope? What does that
mean? What happened?

Antelo: We used to be a joyful, contented people. We lived
in harmony with all of the plants and creatures of the rain
forest. Then some strangers came in with big machines
that cut up our beautiful trees. Many animals lost their
homes and became very sick. When we lost our trees, our
hearts turned cold and gray with grief and despair.

Frannie: That's terrible.

Antelo: This area was once filled with trees and plants
and animals. They cleared the entire area.

Rontihowa: When our hearts turned cold and hard, the
rest of us turned to stone as well.

Antelo: When we saw the lively beauty and color of the
butterflies and birds, our hearts turned warm and our

skin soft again. With beautiful colors like that, it makes us feel that there may be some hope again. How can we ever thank you?

Manny: Your turning from stone is thanks enough. We hope to come back and visit you one day, but right now we are going to find the rain forest.

Frannie: Please tell us where you live so we can send you a postcard.

Rontihowa: We used to live among the trees. We no longer have a home.

Anne: Then you must come with us! You will help us find the rain forest, and we will help you to make sure that the trees there are never cut down.

Manny (*consulting his map*): Let's look on the other side of the mountains.

★ *They all follow* MANNY *offstage.*

★ *Blackout*

Scene 8

★ *Further into the rain forest. The group enters the stage.*

Frannie *(pointing out to the audience)*: Look, everyone! The river! Look at it! It's beautiful. All of the rivers back home are brown and polluted.

Anne and **Gilbert** *(amazed, looking out at the river)*: Wow!

Manny: Look at all the plants and trees!

Rontihowa: This is the perfect spot! We can rebuild our homes with respect for all of nature living together.

Manny: How can people cut down these beautiful trees? We have to tell everyone back home about this place and how important it is that all living things—people, animals, trees, and plants—live together with respect. It's up to us. Humans are the only ones who can make a difference. Where's the camera, honey?

Frannie: I gave it to Gilbert.

Gilbert: I don't have it. I gave it to Anne.

Anne: Me? I never get to hold the camera. Dad is always afraid I'm going to drop it.

Gilbert: Well, don't look at me. I don't have it.

Manny: This is just great! We have this adventure and we have nothing to show for it!

Frannie: Oh, yes we do! Just look around. This is what we have to show! We can make a difference. We can help!

Gilbert: How can we help from all the way back home?

Frannie: Well, they say that the trees are cut down to make paper goods. If we start to recycle our paper, maybe they won't need to cut down so many new trees. And if we do our part, maybe people all over the world will pitch in and do their part as well. Pictures and showing off to neighbors, that's silly. What is important is the rain forest and all of its creatures!

★ *Blackout*

Scene 9

★ *The set of* The Chris Dayton Show. *CHRIS DAYTON enters with a microphone. GLADYS and GEORGE MONTROSE and FRANNIE and MANNY KANE are seated in chairs placed on the stage. CHRIS might take her place in the audience, as on a TV talk show. She pretends that the audience for this play is indeed the audience for her talk show.*

Chris: If you're just joining us, today we're talking travel. Vacations. Family vacations! Surveys say that more than fifty-six percent of you are traveling with your kids. Is it worth it? We're going to find out! Meet the Kanes and the Montroses. Both families have recently returned from vacations.

★ *GLADYS and GEORGE are very excited. The KANES look calm and relaxed.*

Gladys: Pedro was our guide to the ancient city.

George: The food was top rate! Can't get anything like it in the States.

Gladys: You know, when they talk, they roll their Rs. *(demonstrating)* Like *r*ed *r*obin *r*ocket! Isn't that cute?

George: I got some great slides of this dance they do around a hat! They actually put a hat on the ground and stomp around it! Don't ya just love it?

Chris *(to the KANES)*: Mr. and Mrs. Kane. You took your family to the South American rain forest. That must have been very exciting. I'm sure you have stories that would put all the experiences we heard about today to shame.

★ *The KANES look at each other.*

Frannie: What's a shame is the state of the rain forest. We could hardly find it.

Manny: People are cutting down all the trees.

Frannie: Did you know there is a recycling program that we have right here in our town? We never even knew about it!

Manny: We do now!

Frannie: Did you know that if everyone in the U.S. recycled their Sunday newspapers, we could save five hundred thousand trees a week here at home!

Manny: That's twenty-six million a year! If we do our part, maybe other countries will do their part too. Then we might not lose so many trees. And the rain forest might become a home to many living creatures once again.

Chris: What about the vacation? Any slides? Was it as wonderful as the Montroses' vacation?

Manny: No slides this trip.

Frannie: Just tourist traps and high prices. We wouldn't recommend it as a vacation spot.

★ *FRANNIE and MANNY look at each other and smile.*

★ *Blackout*

★ *Curtain*

About *Kabuki Gift*

Kabuki Gift is written to be performed in the Kabuki style, mainly in the way that it looks and in its themes of honor and humor. Kabuki is a Japanese theater form that is a combination of music, movement, theater, and pantomime. In Japan, Kabuki theater is traditionally performed only by men. Female characters are played by male actors. This is because when Kabuki theater originated, it was believed that performing was not a respectable or ladylike activity for women. However, *Kabuki Gift* is meant to be performed by male and female actors.

Written with the utmost respect for Japanese culture, *Kabuki Gift* combines the beauty of the Kabuki theater form with some American humor to create a multicultural, fun experience for both performer and audience.

The Characters

Portraying a character who is very different from you can be a challenge. In *Kabuki Gift*, there is the added difficulty of portraying a different culture and historical period. In order for actors to create the most believable and realistic performance possible, they often must research the time and place in which the characters lived. The library is an excellent place to find this information.

Tu-bah is the exalted wise elder of the region. He speaks in a slow, steady manner with a deep voice and is respected by all of the characters in the play. Every time his name is mentioned, all the characters onstage bow respectfully. He is an old man, and might have a beard.

Rum-ti is the elected official of the people. He will do anything to please the citizens of the town, including giving his daughter's hand in marriage to Bah-low, the warrior from the next town, to keep the peace in the region.

Pum-ti is the wife of Rum-ti. She appears faithfully beside her husband at all official ceremonies. She is in charge of all the preparations for her daughter's wedding and is very concerned about doing what is honorable.

Ti-ti is the daughter of Rum-ti and Pum-ti. She is very upset about the wedding arrangement that her father has made. She is torn between her dedication to her family honor and her love for Roe-nye.

Chi is the servant for Rum-ti and his family.

May-nye is a kindhearted doctor who helps the poor and does not charge them for his services. As a result, he too is very poor and owes money to Yen-noh, a mean, stingy rich man.

Qua-nye is the wife of May-nye. She wishes that her husband would make some money. She is very nervous and easily excited.

Roe-nye is their son, and he is in love with Ti-ti. He is concerned with proving his worthiness to Ti-ti's father in the hope that he will win the right to marry her.

Fan-tu is a baker whose only day off is Wednesday. When awakened from her Wednesday sleep, she is very cranky. She does, however, have a soft spot in her heart for true love.

Piti-pan and **Opo-ran** are craftspeople who work very hard to sell their goods.

Bah-low is a warrior from the next town who is brought in to marry Ti-ti. Everyone thinks that he is mean and rough when in fact he is very sensitive and kind.

Tuh-noh is the daughter of Yen-noh and is crazy about sushi. She loves it! She meets Roe-nye and offers to help him find his gift for Ti-ti. They become good friends, and she learns about the many different ways that one person can care about another.

Yen-noh is an old man who is very rich and tight with his money. He has a secret plan to marry off his daughter Tuh-noh to May-nye's son, Roe-nye. His sushi bills are too high.

The Whistling Wind Women are mysterious keepers of the secret of love. They guard it and refuse to share it. They seem angry and dangerous.

Bo is the servant to the Whistling Wind Women. Bo is a little slow and serves the Wind Women faithfully. Bo can be a male or female character.

Day-sol is a traveling bamboo trader. She works hard and travels the region on foot. She is very tired, yet she tries to be helpful.

Koh is her assistant, who is also weary from the road and complains about their working conditions. Koh can be a male or female character.

Roe-mal is the official town pessimist. He always thinks that the worst will happen.

Koh-mie is the official town optimist. She can always spot the good in every situation.

Taffle-si was appointed mayor of the town by Tu-bah.

Aye, Goh, Lah, and **Fie** are the children of Taffle-si. They are restless, hungry, and tired and would much rather be playing games than going to official ceremonies with their father.

Sets and Props

Much of the set in a traditional Kabuki play is made of cutout and painted pieces of wood that represent trees, rocks, and other objects. There are often painted drops hanging at the back of the stage and ornate curtains called *maku*, usually pulled from one side of the stage to the other.

In *Kabuki Gift*, the setting can remain constant throughout the play. The scenery should reflect the Japanese culture expressed in the play. You may create

Japanese screens, or banners with Japanese words written on them. Or you may want to hang a beautiful Japanese kimono or robe by putting a broomstick through the sleeves.

Be creative in the way you decorate your Kabuki stage. Remember that the Kabuki style is simple and elegant. Don't clutter the stage with too many objects. Your actors will need space to move around.

You can put on *Kabuki Gift* anywhere there's a bit of room. The most important thing to do in a space that is not a real stage is to define your acting area. This means you can decide what is onstage and what is offstage. You can use a clothesline to hang a curtain or a blanket for a backdrop. Designate a backstage area where actors cannot be seen by the audience.

Remember, limited resources don't have to be a handicap. Think of them as a challenge to your creativity and let your imagination take over.

Costumes and Makeup

It's fun to pretend that you are someone else. When you add the element of costume and you begin to look like some other character and not like yourself, the fun really begins.

Traditional Kabuki costumes, or *isho*, are very colorful and ornate. All Kabuki costumes are worn in layers. All actors wear an under and outer *kimono* (robe), over which may be worn additional robes and jackets.

One of the most noticeable elements of Kabuki theater is the special makeup. Kabuki makeup is called *kesho*. Each traditional Kabuki role has a set style of makeup. Most traditional makeup has a base of white. It is believed that the white base hides the real person who is the actor and allows the character to come out.

Female characters usually have high black eyebrows, a thin red line under their eyes, and delicate red lips, all on top of the white base. Male characters usually have larger black eyebrows and full red lips, also on the white base. Warriors usually have thick, sweeping black brows and face lines with red highlights.

As with all the visual elements of Kabuki theater, the traditional makeup, although mostly white, black, red, and blue, is bold and stylized.

Cast

Tu-bah, exalted wise elder
Rum-ti, elected official of the people
Pum-ti, his wife
Ti-ti, their daughter
Chi, their servant
May-nye, a doctor
Qua-nye, his wife
Roe-nye, their son
Fan-tu, a baker
Piti-pan, a craftsperson
Opo-ran, a tailor
Yen-noh, a miser
Tuh-noh, his sushi-loving daughter
Bah-low, a warrior
Whistling Wind Woman #1
Whistling Wind Woman #2
Whistling Wind Woman #3
Bo, their attendant
Day-sol, a traveling bamboo trader
Koh, her assistant
Roe-mal, the town cynic
Koh-mie, the town optimist

Taffle-si, appointed mayor*

Aye, Goh, Lah, and Fie, his children*

*These characters are omitted when working with the smaller cast (eight actors).

Optional Smaller Cast

Actor 1—Roe-nye
Actor 2—Tuh-noh, Chi, Piti-pan
Actor 3—Bah-low, Yen-noh, Koh
Actor 4—Ti-ti, Fan-tu, Wind Woman #3
Actor 5—May-nye, Roe-mal
Actor 6—Rum-ti, Bo, Opo-ran
Actor 7—Pum-ti, Tu-bah, Day-sol, Wind Woman #2
Actor 8—Qua-nye, Wind Woman #1, Koh-mie

★*If you have only eight actors, Scene 1 should start with the entrance of the* COMPANY *(page 50). Scene 2 should be skipped.*

Scene 1

★ *The town square. The mayor,* TAFFLE-SI, *and his four children have gathered in the town square. A raised platform sits centerstage.* TAFFLE-SI *and his children stand on the platform.*

Taffle-si *(to himself)*: Where is everyone?

Goh: I'm hungry.

Aye: I want to go home.

Lah: I'm bored!

Fie: When can we leave?

Taffle-si: Honorable children, do not whimper. Honorable children should obey the wishes of their parents.

Fie: What are your wishes, Father?

Taffle-si *(to himself)*: I thought that everyone would be early for such an event. I bet I know where they are. They are all over at the house of Rum-ti. Rum-ti is, after all, the honorable elected official of the people, and I am just the appointed mayor. But I was appointed by the wise town elder, Tu-bah.

All four kids: Ah, Tu-bah, Tu-bah!

★ *Throughout the play, everytime a character mentions the name TU-BAH, all the actors onstage bow with great respect.*

Lah: Papa, why are we here today for this celebration?

Taffle-si: This is the anniversary of our town's founding.

★ *The COMPANY (except ROE-NYE) enters and gathers around the central platform. As they enter, they bow to each other in greeting. RUM-TI, PUM-TI, and TI-TI step onto the platform. RUM-TI begins to address the crowd.*

Rum-ti: Welcome, everyone, to this great celebration. I know that I speak for my family when I say that the people of this town made it the honorable place that it is today and will create the honorable future of our town for our worthy children, as advised by Tu-bah.

All: Ah, Tu-bah, Tu-bah!

Ti-ti: Who is Tu-bah, Mother?

Pum-ti: He is the wisest man in the town.

Ti-ti: Where is he? Point him out to me.

Pum-ti: He is not here, my honorable child; he lives in the house near the bonsai grove. Shhh, your father is going to talk again.

Rum-ti: As elected official of the town, I would like to proceed with the fulfillment of my campaign promises. You will be happy to note that disposable chopsticks shall be outlawed in our worthy town. We have not the trees to spare for such a thing. "Wash and reuse," that is our new motto. *(Looking at his notes)* Number two . . . Our old motto . . . "Use it or lose it" . . . shall be officially replaced. . . . Number three . . .

★ *RUM-TI continues his speech silently as we hear the private conversations of people in the crowd. Those actors onstage not involved in the dialogue watch RUM-TI as if he is still speaking.*

Roe-nye *(running on, to MAY-NYE)*: Father, am I late? Is she here?

May-nye *(pointing to TI-TI)*: She is up there next to her father.

Qua-nye *(to ROE-NYE)*: There's Yen-noh, that stingy miser! How I wish your father didn't owe him so much money. He is always hanging it over our heads.

Roe-nye: One day I will be very rich, Mother, and I will pay off all of Father's debts.

Qua-nye: Your father is most likely the only doctor who is losing money rather than making it!

May-nye: How can I charge the sick for my services? They are poor and need my help.

Qua-nye: We are poor too!

Yen-noh (*walking over to* MAY-NYE *with his daughter,* TUH-NOH): Hello, May-nye. I haven't received your latest loan payment yet.

May-nye: I will have it for you Tuesday, I promise you, Yen-noh.

Yen-noh: I certainly hope so, May-nye. You know I don't mean to sound pushy—

Tuh-noh (*perking up*): Sushi?

Yen-noh: No, dear, not sushi . . .

Tuh-noh: I love sushi! All kinds and shapes and colors and sizes!

Yen-noh: Yes, my daughter, I know. Come along now.

Tuh-noh: Where are we going? Will we have sushi there?

★ YEN-NOH *and* TUH-NOH *exit.*

★ *We hear* RUM-TI *again, as if he had been speaking all along.*

Rum-ti: . . . and as I promised, I will marry my lovely daughter Ti-ti to the warrior Bah-low from the next town to maintain the peace!

Ti-ti (*alarmed*): No, Father!

★ ROE-NYE *bravely comes forward.*

Roe-nye: No! Sir, you cannot give your daughter to the warrior Bah-low from the next town to keep the peace! I love your daughter and wish to marry her!

Rum-ti *(laughing)*: *You?* You are hardly worthy of my daughter. Besides, it is the will of the people that my daughter marry the warrior from the next town to keep the peace.

Ti-ti: No, Father! *(Runs off crying.)*

Pum-ti *(following her)*: Ti-ti, wait!

★ *Blackout*

Scene 2

★ *Same place, immediately following.* ROE-NYE *and the mayor's children are the only ones left onstage.*

Goh: Play the rhyming game with us, Roe-nye!

Roe-nye: My honorable heart is broken.

Lah: Broken!

Aye: Token!

★ *The children hold hands and skip around* ROE-NYE *in a circle.*

Roe-nye: I'm not playing the game! I am too sad!

Lah: Sad!

Aye: Bad!

Goh: Mad!

★ *The children circle again.*

Roe-nye: Honorable friends, my heart is as blue as the setting sun is orange.

Lah: Orange!

★ *The kids cannot rhyme that. They look perplexed.*

Aye: How can we help?

Roe-nye: What can I do to show Ti-ti's father that I am worthy of his daughter?

Lah: Tell him!

Roe-nye: I tried! He said it was the will of the people that Ti-ti marry the warrior Bah-low from the next town to keep the peace.

Fie: You need to show her father that you are worthy!

Lah: How can we show him?

Roe-nye: I can give Ti-ti a gift that would show her honorable father that I am worthy.

Aye: It would have to be a very honorable gift!

Roe-nye: I would be wise to ask the wisest man in the region what gift I should present Ti-ti to prove my worthiness.

Fie: Who is that?

Roe-nye: Tu-bah!

All: Ah, Tu-bah, Tu-bah!

★ *They all bow in respect for* TU-BAH.

★ *Blackout*

Scene 3

★ *The house of* TU-BAH. TU-BAH *stands centerstage, alone. He has an imposing presence. You may also portray* TU-BAH *as a mysterious voice with no actor onstage.*

Tu-bah: Enter, knowledge seeker!

★ *ROE-NYE enters, nervous.*

Roe-nye: Ah, Tu-bah, Tu-bah!

★ *ROE-NYE bows.*

Tu-bah: Sit!

★ *ROE-NYE sits.*

Roe-nye: Exalted wise elder, I must find a gift!

Tu-bah: A gift?

Roe-nye: Yes, your exaltedness!

Tu-bah: Who shall receive it, young son?

Roe-nye: It is for my intended, sir. Ti-ti, daughter of Rum-ti, the elected official of the people.

Tu-bah: And why a gift, young son? Is there to be a celebration?

Roe-nye: I hope there is to be a wedding—mine, to her!

Tu-bah: Do you love her, young son?

Roe-nye: With all my heart.

Tu-bah: And she you?

Roe-nye: Oh, yes! She told me so in her delicate manner.

Tu-bah: What troubles you then?

Roe-nye: Her father, your exalted, intends to marry his daughter to Bah-low, the warrior from the next town, to keep the peace.

Tu-bah: A marriage of convenience.

Roe-nye: I find it very inconvenient. That is why I must present her with a gift so exceptional that her father and everyone else in the town sees that I am most worthy of his daughter's hand in marriage.

Tu-bah: . . . and a gift shall prove this.

Roe-nye: Not just any gift—a very special and honorable gift. This is why I come to you, your exaltedness. I request your suggestion for the most honorable gift.

Tu-bah: There are many fine craftspeople in your town.

Go to them and seek your gift. Maybe you will find something. Above all, follow your heart.

Roe-nye: I thank you, wise exalted elder. Ah, Tu-bah, Tu-bah. *(He bows.)*

★ *Blackout*

Scene 4

★ *The bake shop.* ROE-NYE *enters and calls to the baker.*

Roe-nye: Fan-tu! Are you here? *(Waits for an answer.)* Fan-tu! *(Waits again.)* Fan-tu!

★ *FAN-TU enters, obviously just awakened.*

Fan-tu *(yawning)*: What is it? What do you want?

Roe-nye: You are the finest baker in town! I come to you for a special sweet gift!

Fan-tu *(angrily)*: Do you not know what day it is!?

Roe-nye: I bid your forgiveness, honorable baker. In my excitement I do not know the day.

Fan-tu: It is Wednesday!

Roe-nye: And what is particular about Wednesday?

Fan-tu: It is my day off. I sleep Wednesdays! Oh, the inconvenience of paper walls.

Roe-nye: I am sorry to disrupt your sleep—but this is an emergency! I need a gift for Ti-ti to declare my worthiness to wed her!

Fan-tu: You love Ti-ti?

Roe-nye: With all my heart.

Fan-tu: Then I shall help you. I have a wonderful gift for you to give Ti-ti. I learned this from a Chinese baker. You can write her a fortune to place in a delicious cookie.

Roe-nye: I don't know how to write fortunes!

★ *FAN-TU starts to clap a beat and begins her chant.*

Fan-tu: It is easy. Just follow my lead!
You have the ability to know the higher truth!
Next full moon brings good luck!

★ *ROE-NYE has trouble keeping the beat.*

Roe-nye: *If your thumb is green—wash it again!*

★ *FAN-TU stops clapping and looks at ROE-NYE in disbelief. She decides to try again.*

Fan-tu: *A stranger comes to you from far away!*
Riches and joy to all who come this day!

★ *ROE-NYE is again off beat.*

Roe-nye: *It's a good time to clean your closet!*

Fan-tu: Maybe you should buy her a hat!

★ *Blackout*

Scene 5

★ *The craft-and-tailor shop.*

Roe-nye *(explaining his problem)*: So, you see my dilemma, worthy craftspeople. I must have a gift of great honorability.

Piti-pan: I've a ceramic duck emblazoned in gold.

Roe-nye: Does it fly?

Piti-pan: No, but the eye moves with remarkable naturalness.

Opo-ran: And I have a special scarf woven from the silk of eighty-nine worms that I cultivated myself. I kept them in a bamboo chest and hand fed them leaves! The fabric is smooth and the color a favorite of all the young girls of our town.

Roe-nye: All the young girls like it, do they?

Opo-ran: It is much sought after.

Roe-nye: I thank you for your suggestions, kind providers. I cannot give my love a bird that does not fly. My feelings for Ti-ti cannot be limited by ceramic and gold. And I cannot give her a scarf that has been viewed by many others, for our love has been a beautiful secret

61

that is just for us. I must return to my home to ponder.

★ *ROE-NYE bows and exits.*

★ *Blackout*

Scene 6

★ *The home of* ROE-NYE. ROE-NYE *is speaking to his mother,* QUA-NYE.

Roe-nye: . . . and none of the gifts were right, Mother. They did not capture the spirit of my feelings.

Qua-nye: Where did you expect to get the money to pay for such a gift? You know that all of the money that Father makes must go to pay Yen-noh.

Roe-nye: Why does Father owe that awful man so much money?

Qua-nye: When your father finished his medical lessons, he had no money to purchase the necessary instruments to practice his profession.

Roe-nye: Why did he ask Yen-noh for the money?

Qua-nye: He is the richest man in the town.

★ MAY-NYE *rushes in, nervous.*

May-nye: Family! Has Yen-noh arrived yet? He said he'd arrive at two moons, and it is nearly three! It is not like that man to be late.

Qua-nye: Especially when he is coming for money.

May-nye: I do hope that he is in a more charitable mood than the one he was wearing at the celebration.

Qua-nye: You *do* have his money, don't you, May-nye?

May-nye: I fear not, dear wife!

Qua-nye: I thought you were to collect the medical fees today.

May-nye: I was, but when I went to call for my money, everyone seemed so poor and needy that I could not accept their payments.

Qua-nye: Let us only hope that Yen-noh has such a generous heart as yours.

★ *YEN-NOH enters with his daughter,* TUH-NOH, *who is eating sushi.*

Yen-noh: May-nye, I have come for my money!

May-nye (*very nervous*): I can explain . . .

Yen-noh: Excuses! Excuses don't pay my sushi bills!

Tuh-noh (*still eating*): Sushi!

Yen-noh: Yes, yes, dear daughter, eat your sushi. May-nye, I want to speak with you in private. We must come to a settlement of this debt.

May-nye: Very well. Roe-nye, entertain Tuh-noh.

★ *All exit except for* TUH-NOH *and* ROE-NYE.

★ TUH-NOH *sits down to give her full attention to her food.* ROE-NYE *attempts to make conversation.*

Roe-nye: Nice night.

★ TUH-NOH *doesn't react.*

Roe-nye: Sort of warm out.

★ TUH-NOH *doesn't react.*

Roe-nye: Is your food very good?

Tuh-noh *(realizing that he is speaking to her)*: It's okay. *(She goes back to eating.)*

Roe-nye: You like sushi?

Tuh-noh *(perking up, she is always happy to talk about sushi)*: I LOVE sushi! It is the very best food there is! When I am eating sushi, I can rest assured that I am providing myself with the proteins and essential minerals that are the R.D.A.B.T.B.

Roe-nye: R.D.A.B.T.B.? What does that stand for?

Tuh-noh: Recommended Daily Allowance By Tu-bah.

★ *They bow.*

Both: Ah, Tu-bah, Tu-bah!

Roe-nye: You know Tu-bah?

Tuh-noh: I've met him on three occasions.

Roe-nye: I have met with him only once.

Tuh-noh: On the subject of nourishment?

Roe-nye: No. On the subject of love.

Tuh-noh: I love sushi!

Roe-nye: I love Ti-ti!

Tuh-noh: With rice and soy sauce?

Roe-nye: Ti-ti is not a food. She is the daughter of Rum-ti, the elected official of the people!

Tuh-noh: You love her?

Roe-nye: With all my heart. I wish to marry her!

Tuh-noh: I love sushi! But I do not wish to marry sushi. It must be different. I can see why you sought out the advice of Tu-bah.

Both (*bowing*): Ah, Tu-bah, Tu-bah!

Roe-nye: I went to him for gift suggestions. You see, Ti-ti's father wishes that Ti-ti marry the warrior Bah-low from the next town to keep the peace in the region. Ti-ti doesn't love Bah-low. She loves me.

Tuh-noh: Does she love you like I love sushi or like you love her?

Roe-nye: Like I love her, I assume.

Tuh-noh: How can you be sure? Has she ever mentioned soy sauce in your presence?

Roe-nye: Of course not!

Tuh-noh: What is this gift for?

Roe-nye: To convince her father that I am worthy of his daughter's hand in marriage.

Tuh-noh: What will you buy her?

Roe-nye: That is just my problem. I have visited the fine craftspeople of our town, and I cannot find that which expresses what is in my heart.

Tuh-noh *(alarmed)*: What is in your heart?

Roe-nye: Love is in my heart! Tu-bah says that I should follow my heart!

Both *(bowing)*: Ah, Tu-bah, Tu-bah!

★ *We hear* TU-BAH'S *voice from offstage.*

Tu-bah: Follow your heart! Follow your heart!

Tuh-noh: Maybe you should not limit yourself to the

67

boundaries of this town. I know a bamboo trader who travels through the entire region. This trader could tell us where to find the perfect gift. Come!

★ *They exit.*

★ *MAY-NYE and YEN-NOH enter.*

Yen-noh: So it is settled. You will have my money by this time tomorrow or you will consent to have your son marry my daughter. *(YEN-NOH crosses downstage right to speak directly to the audience, without the other characters hearing.)* I do not need his money! This way I will marry off my daughter and someone else can pay to feed her!

★ *YEN-NOH exits.*

May-nye *(Crosses to the same downstage right spot to speak to the audience.)*: What shall I do? I have no money and my son is in love with Ti-ti!

★ *MAY-NYE exits.*

★ *Blackout*

Scene 7

★ *The house of* RUM-TI. PUM-TI *is altering* TI-TI's *wedding dress.* CHI, *a servant, is standing in the background, waiting.*

Pum-ti: It is the will of the people. You know how your father feels about the will of the people.

Ti-ti: But it is not my will, Mother. I do not love the warrior Bah-low from the next town. I love Roe-nye. He is the one I wish to marry. He is the one I love.

Pum-ti: Think of it as your civic duty . . .

Ti-ti: And if I deny my duty?

Pum-ti *(shocked)*: Ti-ti, that is a highly dishonorable thought.

Ti-ti: I am sorry, Mother. I am out of my head.

Pum-ti *(to her servant,* CHI*)*: Chi, please bring Ti-ti some tea.

Chi: Yes, ma'am.

Pum-ti: And Chi, please bring my cloak.

Chi: Yes, ma'am.

★ *CHI exits.*

Pum-ti: Ti-ti, I wish that it could be different—but it looks like you will be wearing this dress tomorrow as you wed the warrior Bah-low from the next town. Now, I am going to make the preparations.

★ *PUM-TI exits.*

★ *CHI enters with TI-TI's tea.*

Chi: Here is your tea. Drink it slowly. This is the last cup you will have before the marriage cup.

Ti-ti: The marriage cup?

Chi: Yes, you and Bah-low will drink from the same cup of tea to seal your marriage. The marriage is not legal until you share the tea.

Ti-ti: Then I do not want to drink tea! Take this away! With every sip I can only think that I am losing my one true love—Roe-nye. *(She sobs as the lights dim.)*

★ *Blackout*

Scene 8

★ *The road.* DAY-SOL *and* KOH *(the bamboo trader and his assistant) walk on. They are weary from walking. They stop to rest.*

Koh: How much longer is the walk? We must be approaching the next town.

Day-sol: It is over the next hill. It seems the closer the town becomes, the more my feet give way.

Koh: Each year these towns seem to get farther and farther apart.

Day-sol: Such is the life of a traveling bamboo trader.

Koh: Oh, shoot!

★ *They both sigh.*

★ TUH-NOH *and* ROE-NYE *enter calling after them.*

Tuh-noh: Day-sol! Day-sol! I am so glad that we caught up to you!

Day-sol: Ah, Tuh-noh, what a surprise. Your father didn't send you, did he? I promised that I would pay him back on the seventh moon!

Tuh-noh: No, no. I came because my friend needs your help.

Day-sol: I am very sorry, but we are not looking for another tradesperson. It is all I can do to support Koh and myself.

Roe-nye: I am not looking for a job. I am looking for a gift. A special gift to show that I am worthy to marry.

Day-sol: It is not our practice to act as present consultants.

Tuh-noh: He comes from Tu-bah!

All *(bowing)*: Ah, Tu-bah, Tu-bah!

Day-sol: Well, why didn't you say so in the first place? What is it you're looking for?

Roe-nye: I have been to many merchants and cannot find a gift that expresses that which is in my heart.

★ *We hear* TU-BAH's *voice from offstage.*

Tu-bah: Follow your heart. Follow your heart.

Day-sol: I know just the gift. But it is guarded.

Roe-nye *(determined)*: If it is the right gift, an entire army could not guard it from me.

Day-sol: It is guarded by three mysterious women and their equally mysterious attendant, Bo.

Roe-nye: What is it they guard?

Day-sol: The secret of love.

Roe-nye *(excited)*: If I were to give Ti-ti the secret of love, her father would have to let her marry me! Where are these women?

Day-sol: They are very mysterious. They may even be dangerous.

Roe-nye: I am not afraid. Are you afraid, Tuh-noh?

Tuh-noh *(afraid)*: Just how mysterious are these women?

Day-sol: Very mysterious! They are known as the Whistling Wind Women. Their voices whistle a mysterious song.

Roe-nye: Please, lead us to them!

★ *Blackout*

Scene 9

★ *The dwelling of the* WHISTLING WIND WOMEN. *The*
WHISTLING WIND WOMEN are whispering around a small
box in the center of the stage. They perform their
whistling dance. During the dance, TUH-NOH *and* ROE-
NYE *enter and hide in a corner upstage.* WIND WOMAN
#1 notices them and stops the dance.

Wind Woman #1: What have we here? Are you intruders?

Roe-nye: Why, no. We were just passing through on our
way to the next town.

Wind Woman #2 *(not believing them)*: Passing through?

Wind Woman #3: Our dwelling is not on the way to
anywhere.

Wind Woman #2: I don't believe them.

Wind Woman #3: I say we must proceed with caution.

Bo: Would you like me to check them for hidden
thoughts?

Wind Woman #1 *(pretending to be nice)*: That won't be
necessary, Bo. These fine people are our guests. We must
treat them with respect and welcome them to our
dwelling.

Wind Woman #2: Welcome, dear guests.

Wind Woman #3: We are pleased that you could join us.

Wind Woman #2: Won't you join us for a cup of tea?

Wind Woman #1: . . . and a bowl of fresh rice?

Bo: You do eat grains, don't you?

Roe-nye: We are not very hungry.

Tuh-noh: Thank you anyway.

Wind Woman #1: What can we offer you?

Roe-nye: Well, as a matter of fact, you could give me the secret of love. I ask for it only because I need it quite desperately!

Wind Woman #2 *(pointing to the box on the floor)*: Of course, please take it and enjoy!

★ *ROE-NYE moves toward the box they have been floating around. They surround him, not letting him go.*

Wind Woman #3 *(laughing at how they tricked ROE-NYE)*: Now we have you! And we will never let you go.

Wind Woman #1: We will keep you as our servant.

Wind Woman #2: You will spend eternity catering to our every whim!

Tuh-noh (*pleading*): No! You must let him go! He is in love. He wishes to marry. Please release him. Let him go and take me! I have no love—except for sushi. I do love sushi.

★ *The* WHISTLING WIND WOMEN *stop dancing.*

Wind Woman #3: Sushi! We love sushi.

Wind Woman #2: We haven't had good sushi in many, many moons.

Tuh-noh: I have sushi! I never leave home without some.

Wind Woman #1: Then we will make a trade. The boy for your sushi!

Roe-nye: But, Tuh-noh, you love your sushi! You cannot give it up.

Tuh-noh: Here. Take it. Let my friend go free.

★ *The* WHISTLING WIND WOMEN *take the sushi and start to eat it.*

Roe-nye: Tuh-noh, that was very kind. Why did you give away your sushi when you care for it so?

Tuh-noh: I guess that I also care for you—as a good friend. I want you to marry the girl that you love. I think that I am beginning to understand the many different ways that one person can care for another. I care for you as a friend, and Ti-ti loves you.

Roe-nye: I also care for you as a friend, and I love Ti-ti.

Wind Woman #2: And we love this sushi! It's great!

Bo: Where did you get this?

Tuh-noh: A little deli on the lower east side of our town. They owe my father money. I can arrange to have some sent to you weekly.

Wind Woman #3: What will it cost us for this service?

Tuh-noh: You must give Roe-nye the secret of love so he can give it to his love, Ti-ti.

All the Wind Women: It shall be done.

★ *Blackout*

Scene 10

★ *Preparing for the wedding.*

Ti-ti *(speaking directly to the audience)*: What great despair! I am not in love with the warrior. I am torn by my dedication to my father and the people of my town and by my own heart. What can I do? If I deny my father, the town might revolt, and I would dishonor my family name. But if I go through with this wedding, I will dishonor my heart and have to live with heartache for the rest of my life. Why must love be so complicated? Why must politics determine my fate? Why must I be a teenager in love?

★ *TI-TI exits.*

★ *BAH-LOW enters.*

Bah-low *(speaking directly to the audience)*: What great despair! I am an honored warrior. I have won many battles and great lands! When will my town allow me to make my own choices? I was forced into this wedding to keep the peace between two towns. Why must I be the bridge between two governments? This is hardly fair. Why can people not learn to settle their arguments among themselves? Every time there is a confrontation I am sent in to fight. This is a battle that I did not choose. I am sure that the girl is kind—but how do I know if I want to marry her? How will I know if I want to marry anyone? Why does it always rain right after I wash my rickshaw? There are so many questions that must be answered!

★ *Blackout*

Scene 11

★ *The whole company is gathered for the wedding.* TI-TI
and BAH-LOW *stand facing each other on either side of*
RUM-TI. KOH-MIE *and* ROE-MAL *stand downstage left.*
The rest of the company stands in the upstage corners,
watching the ceremony.

Rum-ti *(speaking to the wedding guests)*: As mayor of
the town, it is my great pleasure to welcome you to this,
the wedding of my daughter, Ti-ti, to the warrior Bah-
low from the next town. The marriage will be narrated
by Roe-mal and Koh-mie.

★ *Each character bows as he introduces himself.*

Roe-mal: I am Roe-mal, the town cynic.

Koh-mie: I am Koh-mie, the town optimist. It is a
beautiful day for a wedding. The sun is shining and the
birds are singing.

Roe-mal: Those clouds in the sky may be filled with
rain, and soon we will all be soaked down to our under-
kimonos.

Koh-mie: The bride first bows to her groom. Then the
groom bows to his bride.

★ TI-TI *bows, then* BAH-LOW *bows and stays bent over.*

Roe-mal: I hope that his kimono doesn't split when he bends over. That would be so embarrassing.

★ *BAH-LOW stands upright again.*

Koh-mie: The groom must walk around the bride four times to show that he will protect her from the four corners of the world.

★ *BAH-LOW walks around TI-TI four times.*

Roe-mal: I hope he doesn't get lost.

Koh-mie: Now they must share the tea to seal the marriage.

★ *RUM-TI hands a cup to BAH-LOW. BAH-LOW drinks and passes the cup to TI-TI. Before she can drink, ROE-NYE enters with TUH-NOH. ROE-NYE carries the box containing the secret of love. TUH-NOH carries a card.*

Roe-nye: WAIT!

Rum-ti: What is the meaning of this?

Roe-nye: This marriage cannot take place! I have been on a journey to find a gift—advised by Tu-bah!

All *(bowing)*: Ah, Tu-bah, Tu-bah!

Roe-nye *(to RUM-TI)*: I have been searching for a gift that would prove to you that I am worthy of wedding your daughter. I have searched far and wide for just the

81

right gift that would express that which is in my heart, and I have found it! I present this to you, Ti-ti. It is the secret of love. I am sure that you know this secret, for I will always be in love with you.

★ *He hands her the box. She opens it and reads the card enclosed.*

Ti-ti: The recipe for sushi à la king.

Tuh-noh: Oh, that's mine! I'm sorry, this must be yours. *(She exchanges cards with TI-TI.)*

Ti-ti *(reading)*: "Follow your heart."

★ *All bow as TU-BAH enters and crosses downstage center.*

Bah-low *(surprised)*: Tu-bah!

All: Ah, Tu-bah, Tu-bah!

Tu-bah: Follow your heart. That is the secret of love.

Bah-low: That is the greatest gift of all. We can give each other crafts and tokens, but true love is a gift of its own.

Tuh-noh *(to BAH-LOW)*: How did you get so smart?

Bah-low: Everyone thinks that I am a fierce warrior. I have a heart and feelings! I enjoy the oceanside at sunset, the moon on an autumn night, and well-seasoned sushi.

Tuh-noh: You like sushi?

Bah-low: I love sushi! I eat it every day!

Tuh-noh: I love sushi, too!

Bah-low: I'm starving!

Tuh-noh: I know a great little all-night sushi place!

★ *BAH-LOW and TUH-NOH start to leave. RUM-TI stops them.*

Rum-ti: What about the wedding?

Bah-low *(to RUM-TI)*: Sir, your daughter should marry the one she loves. She doesn't love me. She cares for Roe-nye, and I do believe it is the will of your people that she marry the one she loves.

★ *Everyone cheers.*

Tu-bah: You see, the gift of love is more valuable than anything. It is the greatest gift of all!

★ *Ti-ti and Roe-nye join hands. All bow.*

★ *Blackout*

★ *Curtain*